Dear Fellow Story Explorers,

Thank you for picking up this extraordinary book! You are holding a unique text, the culmination of many helping hands and one remarkable young author. A young author who participated in an exciting and interactive writing program called Share Your Story! Share Your Story is a nationally acclaimed writing program which mentors aspiring authors through an eight-step writing process. Opportunities to interact virtually with published authors are provided so that participants gain insight and feedback about their new craft! The program concludes with the selection of a participant's story for professional illustration and publication.

Share Your Story addresses barriers that may prevent students from participating in meaningful literacy experiences. It's an integral component of Leap for Literacy's mission to promote literacy, kindness, and a love of reading and writing.

Leap for Literacy offers several initiatives in the Atlanta area, including Read-N-Roll, which uses kindness as the currency for students to build their personal collection of books, and the Read-It-Forward-athon which facilitates schools in partnering with sister schools in at-risk communities to fund new books. You are holding a true labor of love! Please share this powerful book with another Story Explorer and support our mission to create meaningful literacy opportunities for students in our community and across our country.

Yours in Learning,
Stanley T. Tucker
Founder, Leap for Literacy

Go to www.leap for literacy.org to learn about all our programs & how you can get involved

My Home Run Life
Text and illustrations Copyright © 2021 by EJ Sitler. All rights reserved
Printed in the USA. No part of this book may be used or represented in any manner whatsoever without express written permission except in the case of brief quotations embodied in critical articles and reviews.
Book design by Morgan Jennings in partnership with Leap For Literacy Inc

ISBN: 978-1-7366805-6-8

MY H⚾ME RUN LIFE

BY EJ SITLER

ILLUSTRATED BY MORGAN JENNINGS

It was a
cold and windy
day for my first baseball game.

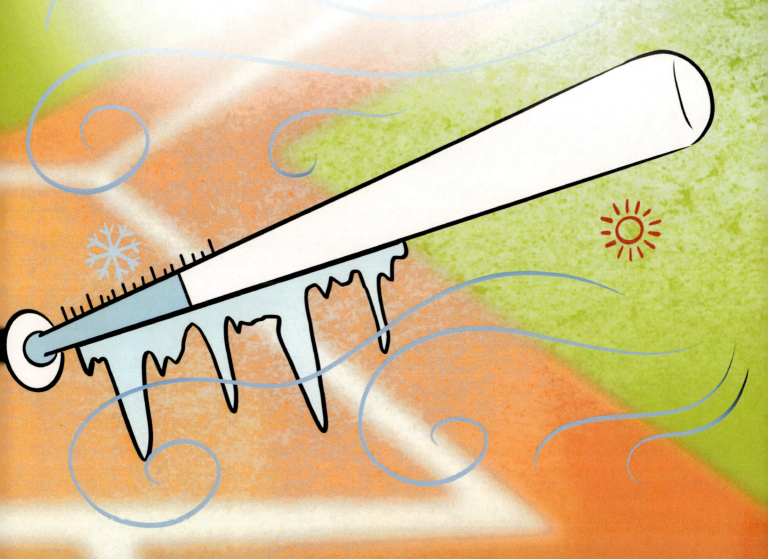

I am on the Phillies' team, and I'm number 19.

Going into the final inning, the game was tied.

It was a nail biter.

Oh no! I thought. I only had one more chance.

If I missed, it would be all over but the crying.

I closed my eyes and took a deep breath. I was ready!

It seemed like the ball was coming at me in slow motion.

I bolted to first base, and the coach gave me the signal to **keep going.**

I rounded second and again saw the coach's sign to keep going! Out of the corner of my eye, I saw the outfielder throw the ball in towards home.

A Note From This Book's Sponsor

This book is sponsored by the Robbins Family
In memory of Staci Michelle Robbins

August 6, 1981 - October 17, 2019

She was a wonderful daughter, a loving sister, a terrific aunt, an incredible educator and writer, and most of all, a role model for the world.

A Peek at the Original Book

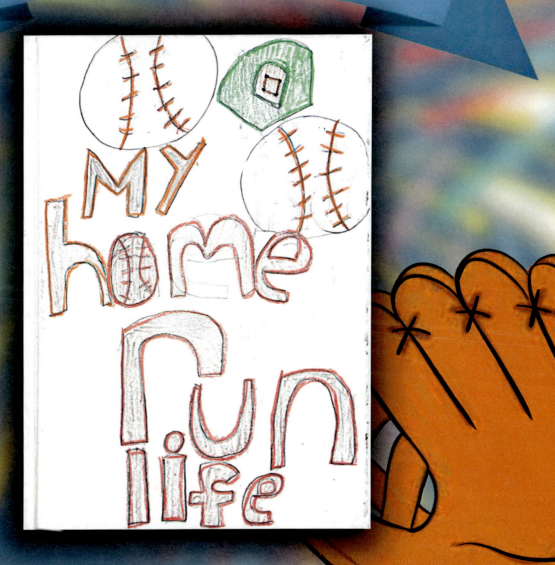

"The crowd was going wild. I could hear my mom screaming 'run EJ run!'"

"It was a nail biter."

Illustrations by the Author

Made in the USA
Las Vegas, NV
19 November 2021